Feed ME WORDS

STORIES BY **KRIS HIRSCHMANN**   ART BY **JAMES K. HINDLE**

Roaring Brook Press
New York

Text copyright © 2016 by Roaring Brook Press
Illustrations copyright © 2016 by Roaring Brook Press
Published by Roaring Brook Press
Roaring Brook Press is a division of Holtzbrinck Publishing Holdings Limited Partnership
175 Fifth Avenue, New York, New York 10010
mackids.com

Library of Congress Cataloging-in-Publication Data
Names: Hirschmann, Kris, 1967– author. | Hindle, James K., illustrator.
Title: Feed me words : 40+ bite-size stories, quizzes, and puzzles
   to make spelling and word use fun! / Stories by Kris Hirschmann ;
   illustrations by James K. Hindle.
Other titles: 40+ bite-size stories, quizzes, and puzzles to make spelling
   and word use fun | Forty plus bite-size stories, quizzes, and puzzles to
   make spelling and word use fun
Description: First Edition. | New York : Roaring Brook Press, [2016] |
   Includes index.
Identifiers: LCCN 2015050311 | ISBN 9781626721739 (hardcover)
Subjects: LCSH: English language—Orthography and spelling—Juvenile
   literature. | Vocabulary—Juvenile literature. | Word games—Juvenile
   literature.
Classification: LCC PE1143 .H47 2016 | DDC 428.1—dc23
LC record available at http://lccn.loc.gov/2015050311

Our books may be purchased in bulk for promotional, educational, or
business use. Please contact your local bookseller or the Macmillan Corporate
and Premium Sales Department at (800) 221-7945 ext. 5442 or by e-mail at
MacmillanSpecialMarkets@macmillan.com.

First edition, 2016
Book design by Andrew Arnold
Color separations by Embassy Graphics
Printed in China by Toppan Leefung Printing Ltd., Dongguan City, Guangdong Province

1   3   5   7   9   10   8   6   4   2

★ Contents ★

★ Introduction ★

When I was a child, words opened up new worlds for me—through the books I read, through the conversations I had with my family and my expanding group of friends, and through my participation in spelling bees. When I was in eighth grade, words took me from my home in Colorado all the way to Washington, D.C., where I won the Scripps National Spelling Bee by correctly spelling the word *elucubrate*, which means "to work out or express by studious effort."

Now, as a father, when I sit down to share a meal with my two children, my aim is to hear all of their thoughts about the world through the specific words they use. My children aren't competitive spellers, but my wife and I have always fostered a love of language in them as they discover their own passions in life. Each hobby or area of interest or study comes with its own vocabulary—those words are the ingredients in a recipe for success. My kids might be talking about fencing or about Minecraft or about something they heard at school that day; regardless, every conversation needs a wealth of special words to go along with it. I love to feed my kids the words they need to keep their minds full of curiosity, growing stronger every day.

The stories and challenges in *Feed Me Words* are meant to make you hungry for knowledge and encourage you to discover the same type of fascination with words that drove me all the way to the national championship when I was a kid. Like cheese sauce covering broccoli, these entertaining stories hide nourishing lessons in spelling, grammar, and vocabulary. Each story and activity offers you a chance to celebrate learning, and share a few laughs along the way.

I hope you enjoy the journey. Happy exploring!

Jacques A. Bailly

Dr. Jacques A. Bailly
Pronouncer for the Scripps National Spelling Bee
Professor of Classics
1980 Scripps National Spelling Bee Champion

Feed
ME
WORDS

Super Salad, Anyone?

Brooke's family was at a restaurant, and it was Brooke's turn to order.

"What would you like for lunch?" the server asked.

"I'll have the turkey sandwich," Brooke replied.

"Good choice! That comes with soup or salad," said the server.

"Okay. That sounds wonderful," Brooke said.

She thought the server would move around the table to take the next order. But he just stood there, staring at Brooke. "Soup or salad?" he repeated.

"Um . . . yes, thank you," Brooke said, puzzled.

The server continued to stare. What could he be waiting for?

"Honey, you have to choose," said Brooke's mom.

"But I *did* choose," Brooke replied. "I want what he said. The super salad."

Brooke was surprised when everyone, even the server, laughed kindly.

"Now I get it," the server said. "I meant S-O-U-P O-R, not S-U-P-E-R. I talk too fast! Would you like soup"—he paused—"*or* salad?"

Brooke giggled. "Salad, please," she replied.

"You got it," said the server. "And I'll tell the cook to make it extra special for you. One *super* salad, coming right up!"

Spelling Words			
lunch	lunch	*noun*	a meal eaten in the middle of the day
super	SOO-per	*adjective*	very high quality
talk	tawk	*verb*	to say words

Pronunciation: -*or* Words

Pronunciation means the way a word sounds when it is spoken. Different people may pronounce words differently. The server in this story pronounces the word "or" like the suffix "er." His pronunciation causes a misunderstanding.

Here are some more "or" words. In these words, how do *you* pronounce the "or"? Reading them aloud can help you figure it out.

1. color
2. doctor
3. flavor
4. mirror
5. odor
6. savor

Dinner Disaster

Elephants are awful guests.
They **spill** your milk.
They make a mess.
They eat too much.
They don't say "Please."
They toss their corn
And throw their peas.
After dinner, you will see
A **broken** cup . . . or two, or three!
Dirty **dishes**? They won't help.
You'll have to **clean** up by yourself.
And while you're cleaning—what a bore!—
Those elephants will ask for more.
Yes, elephants are awful guests.
Invite some dolphins—they're the best!

ph versus *f*

The words *elephant* and *dolphin* aren't pronounced "elep-hant" and "dolp-hin," of course! They sound like "elefant" and "dolfin." Except in a few compound words, the *ph* combo makes an "f" sound.

All of the words on the following list contain the "f" sound. Fill in the blanks with *ph* or *f* to complete the words.

1. al__abet
2. __oto
3. sa__e
4. cra__ty
5. ty__oon
6. __rase

7. tro__y
8. __loor
9. in__ant
10. sym__ony
11. scar__
12. __orget

Spelling Words

spill	spil	*verb*	to accidentally pour or splash
broken	BROH-kun	*adjective*	damaged or not working
dish	dish	*noun*	vessel for serving food, like a plate or a bowl
clean	kleen	*verb*	to make neat and orderly

Answers: 1. ph, 2. ph, 3. f, 4. f, 5. ph, 6. ph, 7. ph, 8. f, 9. f, 10. ph, 11. f, 12. f

This but Not That

It is Super Secret Letter Day! Rosie can only eat things whose names contain a certain letter. Look at the following list of things Rosie can and cannot eat. Can you figure out the secret letter?

▶ She can have cereal, but not pancakes.
▶ She can have butter, but not toast.
▶ She can have grapes, but not apples.
▶ She can have bread, but not a sandwich.
▶ She can have yogurt, but not cheese.
▶ She can have crackers, but not cookies.
▶ She can have turkey, but not chicken.
▶ She can have rice, but not pasta.
▶ She can have drinks, but not snacks.

So here's the big question:

Can Rosie have ice cream for dessert? Why or why not? Can you name the secret letter?

Answer: The names of the foods Rosie is allowed to eat contain the letter r.
Since ice cream contains an r, Rosie gets her after-dinner treat!

Letter Frequency

The letters of the alphabet are not used equally in English. Some appear much more often than others. Here is the alphabet in order of use, from most to least:

1. e	7. s	13. u	19. y	25. q
2. t	8. r	14. m	20. b	26. z
3. a	9. h	15. f	21. v	
4. o	10. l	16. p	22. k	
5. i	11. d	17. g	23. x	
6. n	12. c	18. w	24. j	

Look at the list. Which letters would probably give Rosie more food choices than *r*? Which letters would probably give her fewer choices?

A Chef in the Family

"Woo-hoo!" Gavin's shout of joy rang through the house.

Caitlyn ran to see what was going on. She found her big brother standing with a letter in his hand. "What's the story?" asked Caitlyn.

"I was accepted at my favorite cooking academy!" Gavin said. "I'm going to be a real chef!"

Caitlyn's face fell. "I'm glad you're happy," she said. "But, Gavin, that school is such a long journey from here, and I hate being stuck in the car for hours. The other academies are closer. Why do you have to go so far away?"

"Because it's the best!" Gavin replied. "I've heard so many great stories about it. Master chefs from all over the world teach classes there. One chef even has his own TV show! I'll learn so much."

"That does sound good," Caitlyn admitted.

"Also," Gavin continued, "the campus is near the beach. It will be awesome to go to the local beaches after class."

"That sounds good, too," said Caitlyn. "Can we have lunch on the beach when I visit you with Mom and Dad?"

"We can have lots of beach lunches," Gavin promised. "And I'll make them for you. With my new cooking skills, I'll be able to create some fantastic food."

"Yay!" said Caitlyn. "I guess I can stand the long journeys if there is a treat at the end. *Two* treats, actually—yummy food and seeing you. I'll miss you, but it sure will be great to have a chef in the family!"

Plural Endings

There are many different ways to change singular nouns into plurals. The most common way is simply to add an *s*. Depending on the word, though, different rules may apply.

Try it yourself! Find a noun in the story that follows each rule.

Rule:	Singular noun:	Plural noun:
Just add *s*	treat	_____
Change a consonant + *y* to the consonant + *ies*	story	_____
Add *s* after a vowel + *y*	journey	_____
Add *es* to a *ch*, *sh*, *ss*, or *x* ending	beach	_____

Answers: treats, stories, journeys, beaches

Spelling Words

academy	uh-CAD-uh-mee	*noun*	a school, usually a private school or one that trains in specific subjects or skills
journey	JUR-nee	*noun*	a trip
beach	beech	*noun*	the shore of a body of water

Foodie Daydreams

It was midday, and Maggie was hungry. "What's for lunch, Mom?" she called across the house.

"I'm busy, sweetie," her mom called back. "Can you make yourself some lunch today?"

"Sure," Maggie replied. "I love to cook!"

Maggie went into the kitchen. Hmm, what should she make? Soup sounded good. Maggie opened a can of soup, poured it into a pan, put the pan on the stove, and turned on the burner.

Maggie waited for the soup to heat up. As she waited, she daydreamed about being a world-class chef someday. "I'm going to be the best cook in the entire country. Or maybe even the universe," she thought. "I'll earn tons of money and start a chain of restaurants. I'll be so famous in this community, they'll throw me a parade whenever I come home to visit."

Maggie was so caught up in her daydream that she didn't notice the soup boiling in the pan. The soup bubbled up and overflowed onto the stove.

"Eek!" cried Maggie. She turned off the burner, grabbed a pot holder, and yanked the pan from the stove. She looked sadly at the sizzling, soupy mess.

"Okay, maybe I'm not ready to be a famous chef quite yet," Maggie thought as she started to clean up. "But I will be. I'll learn. Soup today, super-duper tomorrow!"

★ Spelling Bee Fun Fact ★
The 1962 winning word, *eudaemonic* (yoo-dee-MAHN-ic), means "producing happiness." Daydreaming like Maggie does is usually eudaemonic!

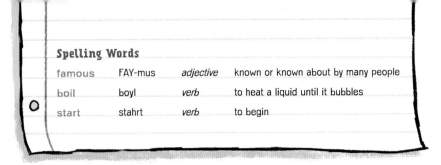

Spelling Words

famous	FAY-mus	*adjective*	known or known about by many people
boil	boyl	*verb*	to heat a liquid until it bubbles
start	stahrt	*verb*	to begin

Parts of Speech: Nouns

Knowing a word's part of speech and definition can help you spell the word. A *noun* is a word that describes a person, a place, a thing, or an idea.

Five of the nouns in this story come from the *Feed Me Words* Index of Spelling Words (pages 85–86). Match each noun with its definition.

1. **pan**
2. **universe**
3. **money**
4. **community**
5. **parade**

a. a public event that involves people marching down a street or riding in cars or on floats or other vehicles in a sequence

b. all of space and everything in it

c. a group of people who live in the same area

d. coins or paper used as payment

e. a container used for cooking

Answers: 1. e, 2. b, 3. d, 4. c, 5. a

Counting on a Snack

The endings *-el* and *-le* sound the same, but good spellers know which is which! Choose the correctly spelled words as you read this story. Do the puzzle at the end to see if you were right.

During a break from his school chorus rehearsal, Liam stood in front of the vending machine. Boy, was he **hungry**! He plugged a (coupel, couple) of quarters into the machine's (panel, panle). He pressed the button for the big (pretzel, pretzle). Nothing happened.

"That's weird," Liam thought. "Maybe the (bagel, bagle) chips will work." Liam pressed the button for the chips. Nope.

"Huh!" he thought. "Maybe just some (bubbel, bubble) gum? It would be better than nothing."

Holding his breath, Liam pressed the button for the gum. Yet again, nothing happened.

"Argh!" Liam cried, frustrated. He leaned against the vending machine, planning to (wiggel, wiggle) it. He hoped he would knock the food loose and it would (tumbel, tumble) down. But before he could start, his chorus teacher walked up.

"This looks like quite a (battel, battle)," said the teacher. "What's up?"

"This machine won't give me a (singel, single) thing," Liam fumed.

"Well, there's a (simpel, simple) reason for that," said the teacher. "Look at the display. It says you've put in fifty cents. You need seventy-five cents. You're twenty-five cents short. Do you have just a little more **money**?"

Liam didn't have any quarters left, but he had plenty of other coins. He pulled out five (nickels, nickles) and put them into the machine. He pressed the button for his first choice, and this time it worked.

"Thanks," Liam said, grinning. "You're the best—and as soon as I eat my snack, I'll be ready to rehearse some more!"

-le versus -el

The word endings *-el* and *-le* can sound exactly the same. This can get confusing! One rule to remember is that the *-le* ending is often used after these letters:

> *b, c, d, f, g, k, p, t, z,*
> and the *st* combination

It is almost never used after these letters:

> *m, n, r, v, w*

The following word search puzzle contains the correctly spelled words from the story. Find all eleven words. Remember, if you can't find a word, you might be spelling it incorrectly. (Note: The words may appear in any order, including backward, upside down, and diagonally.)

```
W  I  G  G  L  E  S  Z
E  P  A  N  E  L  I  X
P  C  L  B  G  B  A  G
V  O  E  W  A  B  G  X
X  U  Z  T  B  U  S  R
A  P  T  B  G  B  I  R
S  L  E  K  C  I  N  H
E  E  R  Z  S  X  G  Z
E  L  P  M  I  S  L  U
R  T  U  M  B  L  E  S
```

Search for the correct spelling of each word:

1. coupel, couple
2. panel, panle
3. pretzel, pretzle
4. bagel, bagle
5. bubbel, bubble
6. wiggel, wiggle
7. tumbel, tumble
8. battel, battle
9. singel, single
10. simpel, simple
11. nickels, nickles

Answers: 1. couple, 2. panel, 3. pretzel, 4. bagel, 5. bubble, 6. wiggle, 7. tumble, 8. battle, 9. single, 10. simple, 11. nickels

Spelling Words			
hungry	HUN-gree	*adjective*	uncomfortable because of a need for food
money	MUN-ee	*noun*	coins or paper used as payment

Getting Warmer

Julia was late to **breakfast** one morning. "My food is cold," she complained.

"I'll take care of that," said Julia's brother, Thomas. "I can change COLD to WARM in just five steps. Watch!"

Thomas carried Julia's plate to the kitchen counter.

"One: I put the COLD food into the microwave," he said.

He slid the plate into the microwave.

"Two: I make sure the CORD is plugged in," he said.

He checked the cord.

"Three: I say the magic WORD."

He then shouted, "Alakazam!"

"Four: I wiggle like a WORM while I press the button."

Thomas wiggled and **jiggled** as he started the microwave.

"Five: I open the door. Here is your WARM food," he said, pulling Julia's steaming plate from the microwave. "See? COLD to WARM!"

Julia giggled as she started to eat. "Very **clever**, Thomas," she said. "Now watch what I can do. I'm about to change *hungry* to *full*—and I don't need any spelling tricks to do it!"

14

Spelling Words

breakfast	BREK-fust	*noun*	the first meal of the day, usually eaten in the morning
jiggle	JIG-ul	*verb*	move with quick little shakes
clever	KLEH-vur	*adjective*	smart and witty

Word Ladders, #1

Word ladders are a type of spelling puzzle. You start with a word and change one letter at a time to make a different word. Here is Thomas's word ladder:

COLD – CORD – WORD – WORM – WARM

Can you complete the following easy word ladders? (Hint: Sometimes there is more than one way to complete a word ladder. If you find a path different from the one given in the answer key, that's fine.)

1. **BUN** – _ _ _ – **NUT**
2. **HOT** – _ _ _ – **DOG**
3. **GLUE** – _ _ _ _ – **PLUM**
4. **HOPE** – _ _ _ _ – **RIPE**

Answers:
1. BUN – BUT – NUT
2. HOT – DOT – DOG
3. GLUE – GLUM – PLUM
4. HOPE – ROPE – RIPE

★ **Spelling Bee Fun Fact** ★
Finalists at the Scripps National Spelling Bee have exactly two minutes to correctly spell their assigned word, beginning as soon as the official pronouncer first pronounces the word.

Spelling Stumper

Chang was excited! His birthday was coming. He was planning a big party with cake, ice cream, and lots of pals.

"I think Saturday **afternoon** would be good," Chang thought. "But I'm not sure. I'd better check to see if I have a softball game."

Chang turned on the computer. He typed C-A-L-E-N-D-E-R into the search box. A message popped up: *No results found*.

Chang **frowned**. "Huh?" he thought. "That's weird."

He typed the word again, being **careful** with every letter: C-A-L-E-N-D-E-R.

No results found.

"This computer has a problem," he grumbled.

"I think your spelling might be the problem," said Chang's dad, who had just entered the room. "Why don't you try it this way?"

C-A-L-E-N-D-A-R, typed Chang's dad.

Poof! The calendar opened on the screen.

"See? There's your calendar," said Chang's dad. "And Saturday afternoon looks like the perfect time for a party."

"Yay! Let's put it on the C-A-L-E-N-D-A-R," Chang said. "Cake and ice cream, here I come!"

-ar Endings

The -ar word ending is not used a lot in English, but it is found in some common nouns. *Calendar* is one example. Other examples include *altar*, *grammar*, *collar*, *dollar*, and *caterpillar*. These words are often misspelled because the -ar ending can sound just like "er."

Fill in the letters to complete the following common -ar words.

1. h a _ _ a r
2. n e _ _ a r
3. b e _ _ a r
4. g u _ _ a r

Spelling Words

afternoon	af-tur-NOON	noun	daytime between 12 o'clock noon and evening
frown	froun	verb	to look upset or angry
careful	KAYR-ful	adjective	done with caution

A Pair of Pears

Lena was shopping for **groceries** with her mom. She was happy because she had a special job to do. She always got to choose the fruit all by herself.

Lena's mom handed her a list. "Here's what we need," she said.

Lena walked **toward** the fruit section.

"Oh! I forgot one thing!" her mom called after her. "**Remember** to get pears!"

"Okay, Mom," Lena replied. "I'm on it!"

In the fruit section, Lena looked at her list:

▶ Apples
▶ Bananas
▶ Oranges
▶ Peaches

Lena got everything on the list. Then she returned to her mom. Her mom looked at the fruit and frowned.

"Where are the pears?" she asked.

"Huh?" Lena said, puzzled. "They're right here. Two apples, two bananas, two oranges, and two peaches. Pairs."

Lena's mom started to laugh.

"I meant P-E-A-R-S, **funny** girl, not P-A-I-R-S," she said. Lena laughed, too.

"I get it now! I'll go back and get some P-E-A-R-S," she replied.

"Thank you, Lena," said her mom. "You're a good shopper . . . and a good speller, too!"

PEARS

Spelling Words

groceries	GROH-suh-reez	*plural noun*	food and other items available for purchase in a store
toward	TOH-urd	*preposition*	in the direction of a specific point
remember	ree-MEM-bur	*verb*	to recall something you previously knew
funny	FUN-ee	*adjective*	having the ability to make someone laugh

Homonyms, #1

Words that sound alike but have different meanings are called homonyms. (They can also be called homophones, if they have the same spellings—but the Scripps National Spelling Bee still refers to them as homonyms.) In this story, the words *pear* and *pair* are homonyms. Even though these words are not spelled the same way, they sound exactly alike.

Can you think of a homonym for each of the following words?

1. **sighed**
2. **eight**
3. **tee**
4. **blew**
5. **flee**
6. **made**

★ **Spelling Bee Fun Fact** ★
Five times in the history of the Scripps National Spelling Bee, the competition has ended in a tie between two co-champions. They were just too good! The word *tie* is a homonym. Can you think of another meaning of *tie*?

Answers: 1. side, 2. ate, 3. tea, 4. blue, 5. flea, 6. maid

Cookie Monster

At the school bake sale, Josef saw his classmate Jenna standing behind a table. On the table sat the most delicious-looking cookies Josef had ever seen!

Josef walked over and stopped at Jenna's table.

"Those are awesome! Did you bake them yourself? Where did you learn how to do that?" he asked.

Jenna smiled proudly. "Yes, I baked them myself. I learned how from my grandma," she said. "Would you like to try one?"

"Yes, please! I bet they're great!" said Josef. He tried a cookie. It tasted just as good as it looked. It was so good, in fact, that Josef couldn't stop himself. He reached for a second sample.

"Hey, stop it!" Jenna laughed. "I have to sell those!"

"Oops! Sorry," Josef said. He pulled some coins out of his pocket and handed them to Jenna. "One cookie, please. That's all I can afford—but don't let any of the others go to waste. If you have leftovers, come find me."

"You got it. They won't be wasted, I promise," Jenna said. "Now get out of here, cookie monster. I have a job to do!"

Past Tense

There are many different ways to change present-tense verbs into the past tense. The basic rule is simply to add -ed. Depending on the word, though, different rules may apply.

Try it yourself! Find a verb in the story that follows each rule.

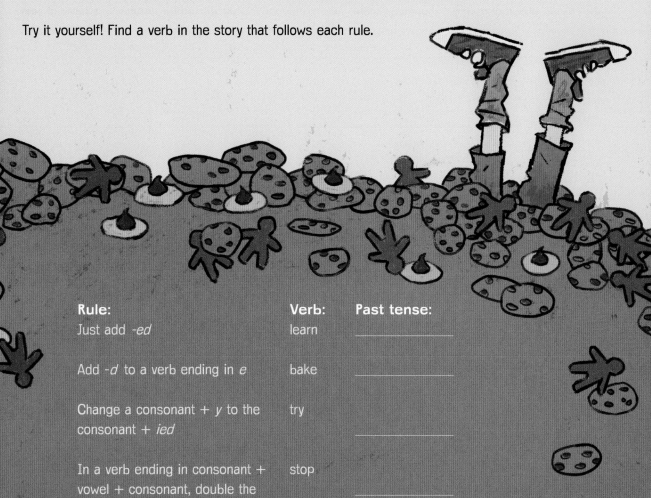

Rule:	Verb:	Past tense:
Just add -ed	learn	_____
Add -d to a verb ending in e	bake	_____
Change a consonant + y to the consonant + ied	try	_____
In a verb ending in consonant + vowel + consonant, double the final consonant and add -ed	stop	_____

Spelling Words

bake	bayk	*verb*	to cook in an oven
waste	wayst	*noun*	unnecessary loss of something
promise	PRAH-mis	*verb*	to say to someone that you will definitely follow through on something
monster	MAHN-stur	*noun*	a strange and sometimes scary imaginary creature

Answers: learned, baked, tried, stopped

When Hunger Comes Knocking

It's Halloween. The moon is bright.
What costumes might you see tonight?
Then . . . a knock! Who is there?
A knight is standing on your stair.
It's your brother in disguise.
You know him by his sleepy eyes.
He yawns, although he wears a grin,
So turn the knob and let him in.
He drops his knapsack on the ground.
Candy later . . . dinner now!
Knead some bread for this brave squire
    While he kneels beside the fire.
    Use a knife to cut his meat
    As he nods off from the heat.
        Plump some pillows for his head,
        Then let him tumble into bed.
           He'll be knocked out, sleeping tight.
           What a warm, full, happy knight!

kn- Words

Many words in this poem contain the *kn* combination. In most uses of this combination, and almost always when it begins a word, the letter *k* is silent. This means that the letters *kn* make an "n" sound.

All of the words on the following list start with the "n" sound. Fill in the blanks with *kn* or *n* to complete the words.

1. __otted
2. __owledge
3. __ourish
4. __obby
5. __imble
6. __ail

7. __uckle
8. __acho
9. __own
10. __ockout
11. __ever
12. __ostrils

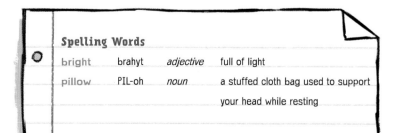

Spelling Words

| bright | brahyt | *adjective* | full of light |
| pillow | PIL-oh | *noun* | a stuffed cloth bag used to support your head while resting |

Answers: 1. kn, 2. kn, 3. n, 4. kn, 5. n, 6. n, 7. kn, 8. n, 9. kn, 10. kn, 11. n, 12. n

Libby's Labels

It is Super Secret Letter Day again! This time, it's all about letter combinations and patterns. Libby is helping out in her uncle's grocery store. He has asked her to assign price labels to items whose names contain a certain letter pattern. Can you figure out what it is?

- ▶ She must label meatballs, but not hamburger.
- ▶ She must label berries, but not melon.
- ▶ She must label butter, but not jam.
- ▶ She must label pizza, but not pasta.
- ▶ She must label waffles, but not syrup.
- ▶ She must label lettuce, but not tomatoes.
- ▶ She must label burritos, but not tacos.
- ▶ She must label pepper, but not salt.
- ▶ She must label eggs, but not bacon.
- ▶ She must label curry, but not sushi.

Libby has one simple question: Which ice cream should she label, the vanilla or the chocolate? Explain your choice. Can you name the secret letter pattern?

Double Consonants, #1

A consonant is any letter that is not a vowel. When the same consonant occurs twice in a row in a word, it is called a double consonant. Double consonants are tricky because they stand for just one sound. For instance, in the word *waffles*, the double consonant *ff* sounds like one *f*.

Look at the following list. Which correctly spelled words have double consonants?

1. **tofee**   **toffee**
2. **tuna**   **tunna**
3. **macaroni**   **maccaroni**
4. **apetizer**   **appetizer**
5. **mufin**   **muffin**
6. **sallad**   **salad**

Spelling Words			
store	stohr	*noun*	a business where you can buy things
label	LAY-bul	*noun*	a tag used to identify and describe an item
melon	MEL-un	*noun*	a large round fruit with a hard skin

Mealtime at the Zoo

Zach loved it when his mom took him to his favorite place—the zoo! Zach liked to look at all the animals.

He especially enjoyed watching the animals eat. It was fun to see so many different creatures gobbling down their food.

Today, Zach went to see the giraffes first. The giraffes were using their flexible lips and long tongues to pluck leaves from trees. They ate a lot of leaves!

Next, Zach visited the koalas. The koalas were eating leaves, too. They pulled the leaves from branches with their long fingers.

When Zach got tired of watching the koalas, he went to see the pandas. The pandas were munching on bamboo shoots. Zach could hear the *crunch, crunch!* as the pandas chewed their tough treats.

Finally, Zach went to see the parrots. The parrots were enjoying a snack of seeds. The parrots cracked the shells with their curved beaks to reach the tasty nuts inside.

After watching the parrots, Zach said to his mother, "Seeing all these animals eating is making me hungry."

"Me, too," Zach's mother agreed. "Let's grab some lunch. It's mealtime for everyone, not just the animals!"

★ **Spelling Bee Fun Fact** ★

Some words sound like what they mean: words like *tweet*, *buzz*, and *whoosh*. These words are called "imitative words" because they copy a sound. The fancy name for these words is *onomatopoeia* (ah-nuh-mah-tuh-PEE-uh). Lots of animal sounds are onomatopoeia. Can you think of more? How about the sound a cat makes? Or a frog?

Plural Nouns

Knowing a word's part of speech and definition can help you spell the word. A *plural noun* is a word that describes more than one person, place, thing, or idea.

The story you just read contains six plural nouns from the *Feed Me Words* Index of Spelling Words (pages 85–86). Match the plural nouns with their definitions.

1. **creatures**
2. **giraffes**
3. **trees**
4. **koalas**
5. **pandas**
6. **parrots**

a. large Chinese mammals that look like black-and-white bears
b. colorful tropical birds that can mimic human speech or sounds
c. large African mammals with very long necks and large red or brown spots on their cream-colored hair
d. animals in general
e. slow-moving Australian marsupial animals that live in trees and have gray fur and big, hairy ears
f. tall woody plants with trunks and branches

Spelling Words

different	DIF-rent	*adjective*	not the same
snack	snak	*noun*	a bit of food eaten between meals

Kung-Food Fighting

Is it *g* or *j*? Answer this question while reading this story! Choose the correct spellings; then check yourself by doing the word search puzzle.

Jackson and Levi were munching on fruit one day on the way to karate practice. Levi finished his banana and tossed the peel into the air.

"Hi-ya! Hi-ya!" he yelled. He chopped at the flying peel with his hand. "I'm a fruit (ninga, ninja)!"

"You're (dangerous, danjerous), is what you are," said Jackson as the banana peel fell to the ground. "Pick that thing up! People could slip on it and (ingure, injure) themselves. And I don't have a spare (bandage, bandaje) on me right now." He laughed.

"You're no fun," Levi pouted. "But okay, you're right."

Levi picked up the banana peel and tossed it into a nearby (garbage, garbaje) can.

"That peel was the (obgect, object) of my fury," he grouched. "How will I show my (magor, major) skills now?"

"Save it for class," Jackson replied. "I'm sure the teacher will (engoy, enjoy) it."

"You're right!" Levi said, his face brightening. "It's a good thing I ate that banana. I'm going to need a (giant, jiant) amount of (energy, enerjy) today. This fruit-powered fighter is ready to chop up all the competition!"

g versus j

In English, the letter *g* sometimes has a "j" sound. This pronunciation is called a soft *g*. The general rule (although there are exceptions) is that when the letter *g* meets the vowel *e, i,* or *y*, the sound is soft.

This word search puzzle contains the correctly spelled *g* and *j* words from the story. Find all ten words. Remember, if you can't find a word, you might be spelling it incorrectly.

T	D	R	M	A	J	O	R
B	A	N	D	A	G	E	A
E	N	E	R	G	Y	S	B
R	G	T	R	U	I	N	L
V	E	A	O	U	I	S	D
J	R	N	B	N	J	O	H
R	O	J	J	R	J	N	F
Q	U	A	E	O	A	H	I
T	S	R	C	N	Y	G	Y
Z	G	E	T	N	A	I	G

Search for the correct spelling of each word:

1. ninga, ninja
2. dangerous, danjerous
3. ingure, injure
4. bandage, bandaje
5. garbage, garbaje
6. obgect, object
7. magor, major
8. engoy, enjoy
9. giant, jiant
10. energy, enerjy

Spelling Words

fruit	froot	*noun*	a usually sweet food that grows on a tree or bush
chop	chahp	*verb*	to cut into pieces

Food Truck Adventure

"I don't feel like cooking," Maria's mom announced one evening. "I heard there's a food truck event downtown tonight. Let's go check it out!"

Maria's family piled into the car. As everyone buckled up, Maria's mom passed her cell phone into the backseat.

"I'm not exactly sure where I'm going," said Maria's mom. "Maria, can you pull up the GPS while I drive? We're looking for Circle Street."

"Sure, Mom," said Maria. She opened the GPS app. S-I-R-K-L-E S-T-R-E-E-T, she typed. Nothing came up.

"Uh, Mom? According to this thing, that street doesn't exist," Maria said.

"Let me look at it," said Maria's brother, Sean.

Maria passed the phone to Sean. He glanced at what Maria had typed, and grinned.

"I think I see the trouble," he said. "Let's try a different spelling."

C-I-R-C-L-E S-T-R-E-E-T, he typed—and a map popped up on the screen.

"There it is. It's just a short distance away, across the bridge. Food trucks, here we come!" he said.

"Thanks, Sean," said Maria. "We could have gone in a C-I-R-C-L-E around this city for hours without your help. Good spelling sure is handy . . . especially when it helps you find food!"

★ Spelling Bee Fun Fact ★
The finals of the Scripps National Spelling Bee are held every year near America's capital city, Washington, D.C.

Consonants: Hard versus Soft

English spelling can be very tricky, and the word *circle* is a great example! It includes one soft *c* (pronounced like "s") and one hard *c* (pronounced like "k").

Here are some more words that present hard versus soft challenges. Point out the "double duty" letter in each word. Identify the sounds each of those letters makes.

1. **garage**
2. **sighs**
3. **cancel**
4. **circus**
5. **grunge**
6. **sausages** *(Hint: There are three s's in this word. Two have the same sound.)*

Answers: 1. g makes the "k" and "j" sounds. 2. s makes the "s" and "z" sounds. 3. c makes the "s" and "k" sounds. 4. c makes the "s" and "k" sounds. 5. g makes the "g" and "j" sounds. 6. s makes the "s" and "z" sounds.

A Perfect Picnic

The weather was perfect for a **picnic**! Grace and her friend Aisha packed a basket full of goodies and headed to a nearby field. They spread a **blanket** on the ground and settled down to enjoy their feast.

But then . . .

"Ewww!" cried Aisha. She brushed a crawling bug off the bun she was about to eat.

The girls looked around. Bugs were crawling everywhere! The **greedy** visitors were swarming around the picnic basket.

"I'll take care of it," said Grace. "I won't let those BUGS BITE our food!"

Grace jumped to her feet.

"One: Let's get those BUGS away from the BUNS!" she said.

Grace shooed the bugs away.

"Two: I'll place the BUNS in these plastic BINS."

She worked as she spoke, tucking the buns away.

"Three: I'll also put all these other BITS of food in there. Too bad, bugs!"

Grace glared at the insects.

"Four: The food is safe. Those bugs can't BITE it now," Grace said proudly.

Aisha grinned from ear to ear. "That was fantastic, Grace!" she said. "Now that the BUGS can't BITE, our food is safe. But I don't know about my legs. There are still a lot of bugs around here. Let's find a better spot for our picnic . . . and then let's eat!"

Word Ladders, #2

Grace made a word ladder to change the word BUGS into BITE. Here is Grace's word ladder:

BUGS — BUNS — BINS — BITS — BITE

Can you complete the following word ladders?

1. PIE — _ _ _ — _ _ _ — PEA
2. FARM — _ _ _ _ — _ _ _ _ — FOOD
3. MORE — _ _ _ _ — _ _ _ _ — CAKE
4. DESK — _ _ _ _ — _ _ _ _ — FISH

Spelling Words

picnic	PIK-nik	*noun*	a meal eaten outdoors, or a party involving an outdoor meal
blanket	BLAYN-kit	*noun*	a sheet of fabric used for warmth
greedy	GREE-dee	*adjective*	selfishly wanting more

Answers:
1. PIE — PIT — PET — PEA
2. FARM — FORM — FORD — FOOD
3. MORE — CORE — CARE — CAKE
4. DESK — DISK — DISH — FISH

Campfire Cuisine

Taye and his uncle were camping in the **forest** one weekend. They had been busy outdoors all day, and now Taye was ready to eat.

"I'm dying for dinner," he said. "Let's grill some hot dogs."

"We aren't grilling anything quite yet," Taye's uncle replied. "I have to chop some wood first and make a fire."

"That will take a long time," Taye groaned. "I really might die of hunger!"

"I'm pretty sure you'll live," laughed Taye's uncle. "And anyway, the work will go quickly if you help. You can **scrape** that dirty grill while I'm chopping."

"Okay," Taye said as he settled down to his task. "I'm scraping it. I'll make it **sparkle**."

Sure enough, the grill was soon sparkly and clean.

As Taye finished, his uncle walked over with a big armful of firewood.

"Great job!" his uncle said. "I'll start the fire. Taye, please grab the hot dogs."

Taye opened the cooler. He dug through the food inside, but there were no hot dogs. "Uh, did we **forget** them?" he asked. "I don't see any hot dogs. But we do have hamburgers."

Taye's uncle slapped his forehead and sighed. "I'm always forgetting something," he said. "I'm sorry about the hot dogs, but hamburgers are good, too. Anything cooked over a campfire sounds great to me. Let's get grilling!"

Present Participles

Verbs that end in *-ing* are called present participles. They describe actions that are happening in the present moment.

Here are five rules for adding the *-ing* ending:

1. Most verbs: just add *-ing*.
2. Most verbs ending in silent *e*: remove the *e* and add *-ing*.
3. Most verbs ending in consonant + vowel + consonant: double the final consonant and add *-ing*.
4. Verbs ending in *ie*: change to *ying*.
5. Do not double the final consonant when the verb ends in *w*, *x*, or *y*.

Follow the rules to add the *-ing* ending to the following verbs:

1. **lie**
2. **raise**
3. **allow**
4. **eat**
5. **cook**
6. **like**
7. **tie**
8. **control**
9. **plan**
10. **relax**

Answers: 1. lying, 2. raising, 3. allowing, 4. eating, 5. cooking, 6. liking, 7. tying, 8. controlling, 9. planning, 10. relaxing

Spelling Words

forest	FOR-ist	*noun*	a large area of trees
scrape	skrayp	*verb*	to move against something rough
sparkle	SPAHR-kul	*verb*	to produce small flashes of light or sparks
forget	for-GET	*verb*	to not be able to think of or remember

Hot and Cold

Malik entered his house one evening after a long soccer practice. Right away, a delicious smell tickled his nose. Yum! Malik followed the scent to the kitchen. He found his dad by the stove, stirring something in an enormous pot.

"I'm starving!" Malik announced. "What's for dinner?"

"It's chili," said Malik's dad.

"What?" said Malik. "That doesn't look chilly to me. I see steam coming out of the pot. It looks hot."

"It *is* hot," replied Malik's dad. "It's boiling hot."

"But you just said it was cold," Malik said, confused. "I don't get it."

Malik's dad started to laugh. "I didn't say it was cold," he responded. "I said it was chili. C-H-I-L-I, not C-H-I-L-L-Y."

"Oh! That makes more sense!" Malik said happily. "I love C-H-I-L-I, and from the size of that pot, I'm guessing there's plenty of it. Thanks, Dad. I can't wait to chow down on some hot food!"

Word Origins

Sometimes foreign foods become popular in English-speaking countries. When they do, their names often become part of the English language. The word *chili*, for example, comes from Mexican Spanish. It has been used since the 1500s to describe a type of red pepper. The word now also refers to a tasty dish flavored with chili peppers.

Although *chili* comes from Spanish, many English food words that end in *i* come from Italian. Examples include *spaghetti*, *salami*, and *ziti*. How many other Italian favorites ending in *i* can you name? Can you name any food words ending in *i* that come from other countries?

Examples: ravioli, broccoli, kiwi, sushi

Spelling Words

enormous	ee-NOR-mus	*adjective*	very large
chilly	CHIL-ee	*adjective*	cold or cool

A Chef's Utensils

It is Super Secret Letter Day again! Owen is working in the kitchen. He can only use tools and utensils whose names contain a certain letter. Look at this list of things Owen can and cannot use. Can you figure out the secret letter?

- He can use forks, but not knives.
- He can use pots, but not pans.
- He can use bowls, but not plates.
- He can use bottles, but not cups.
- He can use tongs, but not trays.
- He can use the chopper, but not the grater.
- He can use the toaster, but not the blender.
- He can use the stove, but not the fridge.
- He can use the microwave, but not the faucet.
- He can use the oven, but not the freezer.

So here's what Owen really wants to know: Can he use cookbooks? Why or why not? Can you name the secret letter?

38

Vowel Frequency

Some letters pop up more often than others in English. Let's take a closer look at just the five vowels. Here's the order of their frequency, from most to least used: *e, a, o, i, u*. You can see that *o* is right in the middle of the list.

But here's a question for you. Without looking back at the letter frequency list on page 7, which do you think are used more often: vowels or consonants?

Answer: The vowels are popular! e, a, o, and i rank among the top five letters. (t is the only consonant to crack the top tier; u is a little farther down the list at number 13—but that's still in the top half. Go, vowels!

Birthday Noodles

"Class, we have a treat today," announced Mikayla's teacher one afternoon. "It is Li's birthday, and Li's mother is here to help us explore a Chinese birthday tradition. So listen up and be polite!"

Everyone clapped as Li's mother stood up. She walked around the classroom, setting a bowl of noodles and chopsticks on the table in front of each student. "These bowls are full of Chinese birthday noodles," Li's mom explained. "The noodles are long, to represent long life. You slurp in the longest noodle you can. It's good luck."

She nodded toward the bowls on the tables.

"Go ahead, taste it," she said.

Mikayla grabbed her chopsticks and plucked one end of a long noodle from the bowl in front of her. She slurped it in . . . and slurped . . . and slurped . . . until she couldn't fit one more bit of noodle in her mouth.

Li's mother saw Mikayla's bulging cheeks. She chuckled. "Now bite the noodle off, chew, and then swallow it," she said. "Otherwise it doesn't count!"

Mikayla did as she was told—although her mouth was so full, it was hard to chew! When she had finally swallowed the giant noodle, she smiled at Li.

"Happy birthday, Li," she said. "May you live for one **hundred** years."

"That noodle was so long, I might get *two* hundred years," Li replied. "Thanks, everyone! I'm so happy you could share my birthday tradition!"

Parts of Speech: Verbs

Knowing a word's part of speech and definition can help you spell the word. A *verb* is a word that describes an action.

The story you just read contains five verbs from the *Feed Me Words* Index of Spelling Words (pages 85–86). Match each verb with its definition.

1. **swallow**   a.   to sense flavor
2. **taste**   b.   to hear and pay attention
3. **listen**   c.   to participate in something with another person or other people
4. **explore**   d.   to put something into your stomach through your mouth and throat
5. **share**   e.   to learn about something by trying it

★ **Spelling Bee Fun Fact** ★

Most of the spellers in the Scripps National Spelling Bee are from the United States, but spellers from other countries have been participating since 1978. Over the years the national stage has hosted spellers from as far away as New Zealand, Ghana, and South Korea.

Spelling Word

hundred   HUN-drid   *noun*   a number equal to ten times ten

The Case of the Missing Candy

What's the rule: *i* before *e* . . . or *e* before *i*? Choose the correct spellings as you read this story. Use your answers to complete the puzzle at the end.

Jayna and her (friend, freind) Lexie were having a snack after school one day when Jayna's brother, Samar, burst into the kitchen. "You two are (thieves, theives)," he declared. "You stole a (piece, peice) of my candy!"

"I did not **steal** it!" Jayna said.

"Me (niether, neither)," Lexie huffed.

"Well, I don't (believe, beleive) you, because it's gone," Samar said.

"Hold on, Samar. I *know* we didn't take it. This is (wierd, weird)," said Jayna. "Let's think for a moment." Jayna stared at the (cieling, ceiling), puzzled.

After a (brief, breif) pause, Jayna smiled. "I think I know who the (thief, theif) is," she said. "Be quiet and listen."

Then they all heard a noise in the other room.

Crinkle, crinkle, crinkle. It was the sound of a candy wrapper—and it was coming from under the couch.

"Benji!" (shrieked, shreiked) Samar. He dove to the floor, reached under the couch, and (siezed, seized) the small brown dog with an unopened candy in its mouth.

"*Phew*, he didn't eat it," Samar said. "That's a (relief, releif). Now I can **relax**. And I **suppose** I owe you an apology."

"It's all right, Samar," Jayna said with a smile. "I'm just **thankful** that Benji is okay. He's a little (mischief, mischeif) maker—but he sure is cute!"

ie versus *ei*

It can be tricky to remember which words are spelled with *ie* and which are spelled with *ei*. There is a famous rule that says, "*i* before *e* except after *c*." This is true in many cases (for instance, *receive*, *deceit*), but not always (*ancient*, *financier*). To be really good at *ie* and *ei*, you have to memorize many words.

This word search puzzle contains the correctly spelled *ie* and *ei* words from the story. Find all thirteen words. Remember, if you can't find a word, you might be spelling it incorrectly.

T	H	V	Y	B	M	C	R	F
H	S	H	R	I	E	K	E	D
I	M	I	P	I	V	I	V	N
E	E	Y	L	W	H	R	E	T
F	P	I	E	C	E	I	I	H
Z	N	I	S	L	T	P	L	I
G	R	I	I	H	S	Y	E	E
D	M	E	E	E	P	F	B	V
H	F	R	I	E	N	D	W	E
O	M	H	D	E	Z	I	E	S

Search for the correct spelling of each word:

1. friend, freind
2. thieves, theives
3. piece, peice
4. niether, neither
5. believe, beleive
6. wierd, weird
7. cieling, ceiling
8. brief, breif
9. thief, theif
10. shrieked, shreiked
11. siezed, seized
12. relief, releif
13. mischief, mischeif

Answers: 1. friend, 2. thieves, 3. piece, 4. neither, 5. believe, 6. weird, 7. ceiling, 8. brief, 9. thief, 10. shrieked, 11. seized, 12. relief, 13. mischief

Spelling Words			
steal	steel	*verb*	to take something that is not yours
relax	re-LAKS	*verb*	to make less stressed or anxious
suppose	suh-POHS	*verb*	to believe something is true or possible
thankful	THAYNK-ful	*adjective*	glad or grateful about something

So Many Questions

Riddle me this, riddle me that!
Why are pancakes always flat?
Why do chopsticks come in pairs?
When can I have lunch upstairs?
Where do rutabagas grow?
Why can't I eat cookie dough?
What's the quickest thing to cook?
Where's the apple that you took?
Which potato should I peel?
Who is coming to this meal?

Hey! Is this a goofy game?
All these riddles start the same!
Take a look and you will see
That every question has a key.
Who, what, which, when, where, and why
Are pretty helpful—that's no lie.
Remember, when you need a clue,
The combo that will WHiz you through!

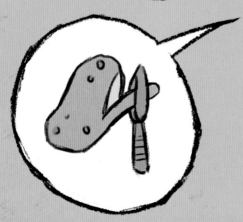

★ Spelling Bee Fun Fact ★

Did you know that you can spell out a letter as a word? All twenty-one consonants—that is, every letter except for *a, e, i, o,* and *u*—have names that can be spelled. One contestant in the finals of the 1998 Scripps National Spelling Bee found that out when she had to spell the word for *h*. How would you spell *h*? The dictionary says it's spelled A-I-T-C-H.

wh- Words

In most *wh-* beginnings, the *h* is silent. You pronounce
the combination like a *w*. Most of the question words in the poem start
with a "w" sound (*what, when, which, where, why*). In a few *wh-* beginnings, the
w is silent. You pronounce the combination like an *h*. One question word in the poem starts
with an "h" sound (*who*).

Look at the following *wh-* words. Which words start with a "w" sound? Which words start with an
"h" sound?

1. **whom**
2. **whack**
3. **wheel**
4. **whole**
5. **whale**
6. **whiff**
7. **whose**
8. **whirl**
9. **white**
10. **whistle**
11. **whoever**
12. **wheat**

Spelling Words			
riddle	RID-ul	*noun*	a puzzling or clever question that is meant to be fun to solve
upstairs	UP-stayrz	*adverb*	at a higher place in a building
quickest	KWIK-ist	*adjective*	the fastest

Read It and Eat

Yum! Jorge's mouth watered as he scanned the menu in his favorite restaurant. There were so many choices. What should he have?

"What are *you* ordering?" he asked his **grandparents**, who were sitting on the other side of the table.

"I don't know," his grandmother replied, frustrated. "I can't find my glasses, so I can't read this menu."

"Sure you can," said Jorge. "Let me help you."

Jorge reached across the table and plucked the menu from his grandmother's hands.

"Is this the MENU you can't read?" he asked. His grandmother nodded.

"All right. **Prepare** for me to MEND your problem," Jorge said.

He reached over and plucked his grandfather's glasses off his head.

"See? Here is a pair of glasses. I'm sure Grandpa will LEND them to you for a moment," he said.

He handed the glasses to his grandmother. She put them on with a grateful smile.

"Let me LEAD your attention back to the menu," Jorge said. He handed the menu back to his grandmother. "Can you READ it now?"

"I can!" his grandmother declared. "I can READ the MENU perfectly . . . and to answer your question, I think I'll have the **daily** special."

"And I'll have the **roast** beef sandwich," Jorge said. "Enough READing. Let's eat!"

Spelling Words

grandparent	GRAND-payr-unt	*noun*	the parent of one's parent
prepare	pree-PAYR	*verb*	to get something ready
daily	DAY-lee	*adjective*	happening every day
roast	rohst	*adjective*	cooked in an oven

Word Ladders, #3

Jorge made a word ladder to change the word MENU into READ. Here is Jorge's word ladder:

MENU – MEND – LEND – LEAD – READ

Can you complete the following word ladders?

1. **BIT –** _ _ _ **–** _ _ _ **– PEA**
2. **MILD –** _ _ _ _ **–** _ _ _ _ **– FOOD**
3. **CODE –** _ _ _ _ **–** _ _ _ _ **– RARE**

Answers:
1. BIT – PIT – PET – PEA
2. MILD – MOLD – FOLD – FOOD
3. CODE – CORE – CARE – RARE

47

"Turnip" the Heat

Eli and his cousin Sam were playing their favorite word-building game one afternoon. The score was close—*too* close. Eli looked at his letter tiles: O, T, I, W, P, H, B. What move could he make to earn a lot of points?

Eli saw that the word TURN was already on the board.

"If I had a U, then I could build T-U-R-N-U-P and earn a triple word score!" he thought.

Right then Sam's sister, Maddie, came up behind Eli. "Can I help?" she asked.

"Sure," Sam said with a chuckle. "Eli needs all the help he can get."

Maddie looked at Eli's tiles. "You have a perfect move," she said. She pointed to the I,

then the P. She leaned close to whisper into Eli's ear. "T-U-R-N-I-P," she said.

"Oh! That's how you spell it?" said Eli. "That's a lucky break!"

Eli placed the I and the P in the proper squares.

"*Ba-da-boom!* Triple word score," he crowed.

"Wow! Good one! And you didn't leave me any moves, either," Sam said with a good-natured grin. "You definitely TURNED UP the competition with that TURNIP. Let's keep playing—and this time, Maddie, you don't get to help. Eli will have to do his own spelling from now on!"

Soundalike Vowels

Vowels can have many different pronunciations. Sometimes this makes it hard to choose the correct vowel.

Look at the following list. Choose the correct vowel for each space.

1. **leftov_r**   *e* or *u*
2. **col_r**   *e* or *o*
3. **must_rd**   *a* or *e*
4. **natur_l**   *a* or *e*
5. **spin_ch**   *a* or *i*
6. **skill_t**   *e* or *i*
7. **app_tite**   *a* or *e*
8. **lett_ce**   *i* or *u*

★ Spelling Bee Fun Fact ★

In the 1975 Scripps National Spelling Bee, the winning word contained a soundalike vowel: *incisor*. An incisor is one of your teeth, and most adults have eight incisors to help cut food.

Spelling Words

build	bild	*verb*	to construct
whisper	WIS-pur	*verb*	to speak extremely quietly
definitely	DEF-in-it-lee	*adverb*	without a doubt; absolutely

A Dainty Tea Party

Anna sipped from her teacup and smiled at her three best friends, who were sitting in a circle around the table with their favorite dolls. She had wanted to throw a special party for everyone— and this party was *extra* special! She had set the table with her mother's very best china. The plates and cups were loaded with tasty snacks and drinks.

"Would you like some more tea, Alisa?" Anna asked her doll. She lifted the teapot.

At that moment, Anna's mother entered the room. "Oh my! Is that my good china?" she gasped. "Anna, that's breakable, and it's not replaceable."

"What does that mean?" Anna asked.

"It means it's possible to break it, and I can't **replace** it if it gets broken," her mother explained. "Sweetie, it's understandable that you want to do something nice for your friends and your dolls. But let's use paper plates and cups, okay?"

"Okay, Mom," said Anna. "I can accept that. I guess that means it's acceptable, right?"

"That's right," her mother said, and smiled. "Thanks for being so reasonable. Everyone, help me put away that china . . . *carefully*. Then we'll get everything you need to **continue** this amazing party!"

Spelling Words

| replace | ri-PLAYS | verb | to put something new in the place of something else |
| continue | kun-TIN-yoo | verb | to keep going |

-able Endings

The ending -*able* turns a verb into an adjective. The adjective means that it is *possible* to *do* the verb. Here's an example: Can you DO it? If yes, then it's DOABLE!

Identify all of the -*able* words in the story. Then add the -*able* ending to the verbs on this list to make common adjectives.

1. **read** + *able* = _____
2. **wash** + *able* = _____
3. **spill** + *able* = _____
4. **pay** + *able* = _____
5. **wear** + *able* = _____

Answers: 1. readable, 2. washable, 3. spillable, 4. payable, 5. wearable

The Salsa Champion

Devin had just returned from competing at the county fair. He felt wonderful! He had worked hard to come up with a great recipe, and he had won first prize in his category. He was so proud that he took his prize ribbon to show to Jake, his best friend.

Devin expected Jake to be happy. But to his surprise, Jake just looked puzzled.

"Wow! I didn't even know they gave prizes for that at the fair," Jake said.

Huh? What was up with that? Maybe Jake was jealous. "Um, yeah. Of course they do," Devin replied. "And I earned it! I mean, I don't want to brag or be boastful, but I really was the best."

"I'm sure you were," Jake said. "But, I mean, I didn't even know you could do that."

Now Devin was getting mad. "Where are your manners?" he snapped. "I did something amazing, and you're just being mean."

"Okay, you're right, I'm sorry," Jake said. "But, Devin—when did you learn how to dance?"

Devin looked at the ribbon.

"First Prize," it read. "Best Salsa."

Devin started to laugh. "Now I get it!" he said. "I won the prize for making delicious salsa, the food. I didn't win a salsa dance contest."

"Well, that's a relief," Jake said, and smiled. "I don't know much about dancing—but I do know how to eat. Let's go have some of that prize-winning salsa right now!"

Homonyms, #2

On page 19, we explained that homonyms are words that sound alike but that have different meanings. Some homonyms are spelled exactly alike. The word *salsa* is one example. It can mean a type of food. It is also a type of dance.

Here are just a few words that have several definitions.
Can you think of any more homonyms?

- ▶ **bat**
- ▶ **rest**
- ▶ **row**
- ▶ **sink**

★ **Spelling Bee Fun Fact** ★

The names of dances make great spelling words, like *salsa*, *ballet*, *jazz*, and even *polka*. What is your favorite dance? Do you know how to spell it? (You're extra lucky if it's the dance associated with the song "Y.M.C.A."— that's an easy one to spell!)

Examples: jam, board, fair.

Spelling Words

brag	brag	*verb*	to talk about yourself or things you have done in an overly proud way
boastful	BOHST-ful	*adjective*	bragging about something you have done, something you have, or something you are
manners	MAN-urz	*plural noun*	the way you behave around other people

Sofia's Secret Ingredients

It is Sofia's turn to figure out Super Secret Letter Day! Sofia is a contestant in a cooking challenge. The challenge has one tricky **detail**: contestants can only use ingredients that contain a certain letter combination. Can you sort out what it is?

- ▶ She can use noodles, but not potatoes.
- ▶ She can use seeds, but not nuts.
- ▶ She can use mushrooms, but not onions.
- ▶ She can use seaweed, but not herbs.
- ▶ She can use beets, but not turnips.
- ▶ She can use roots, but not leaves.
- ▶ She can use green beans, but not black beans.
- ▶ She can use goose, but not turkey.

Sofia is **eager** to impress the judges, and she just has one question: Should she serve iced tea or iced coffee with her dish? What do you think? Can you name the secret combination?

Spelling Words

detail	DEE-tayl	*noun*	a small individual part
eager	EE-gur	*adjective*	very interested and excited

Double Vowels

The vowels *e* and *o* are often doubled in everyday English. Spelling them can be a little tricky because the double vowel *ee* has three soundalikes: *ea*, *ei*, and *ie*. And the double vowel *oo* can make several different sounds. You can hear a few if you say "mood," "good," and "blood" out loud. Yikes!

Look at the following list. Can you pick out the correct spelling of each word?

1. **cookie**   **cookee**
2. **food**   **foud**
3. **beaf**   **beef**
4. **treet**   **treat**
5. **soop**   **soup**

A Breakfast to Impress

One Saturday **morning**, Sam woke to the sound of someone bustling around in the kitchen of his parents' condominium. He got out of bed, yawning, and headed downstairs to check it out.

In the kitchen, Sam found his mother at work. She was frying a mixture of sausages, peppers, and potatoes for breakfast. As Sam watched, his mother lifted the pan and gave it a quick jerk. The sizzling food flew into the air, turned over, and landed—*plop*—right back in the pan.

"Wow! How do you do that?" Sam asked.

"It's an old chef's trick," his mother replied. "You have to push the pan forward and then pull it backward while flipping it upward."

"Neat! Can I try it?" Sam asked.

"Yes, another time," his mother answered. "It takes **practice**, and this food is really hot. I don't want you to burn yourself."

"Me, neither!" Sam agreed. "But I'm glad I got up early to see your trick."

"I'll teach you soon," Sam's mother promised. "In the meantime, go call your father and your sister. Breakfast is served!"

Parts of Speech: Adverbs

Knowing a word's part of speech and definition can help you spell the word. An *adverb* is a word that modifies a verb, an adjective, or another adverb. It usually answers questions like "How?" "Where?" "When?" or "How much?"

The story you just read contains five adverbs from the *Feed Me Words* Index of Spelling Words (pages 85–86). Match each adverb with its definition.

1. **early**
2. **backward**
3. **downstairs**
4. **around**
5. **forward**

a. to the front or the future
b. at a lower place in a building
c. before the time that is expected
d. toward the rear
e. throughout a space; along a curve or circle

★ **Spelling Bee Fun Fact** ★
Although many winning words at the Scripps National Spelling Bee have been nouns and adjectives, none to date has been an adverb.

Answers: 1. c, 2. d, 3. b, 4. e, 5. a

Spelling Words

morning	MOHR-ning	*noun*	the part of the day from dawn until noon
practice	PRAK-tis	*verb*	to train in something in order to gain skill

Vegetable Plotting

Are the words in parentheses spelled with *s* or *z*? Choose the right ones as you read. Do the puzzle at the end to see if you were right.

One spring morning, Angela found her father digging in the backyard with a shovel. "What are you doing, Dad?" she asked him. "Searching for buried (treasure, treazure)?"

"Ha! It could look like that, I (suppose, suppoze)," her father replied. "But no. Now that the winter (freese, freeze) is over, I'm planting a **vegetable** garden. It's a (surprise, surprize) for your mother. Do you want to help me (measure, meazure) the patch?"

"Sure!" said Angela. "What (sise, size) do you want it?"

"Huge!" her father said. "I want to grow a (thousand, thouzand) tomatoes."

"Wow. That's a lot of tomatoes," Angela said. "Are you trying to win a contest or something?"

"Nope," her dad replied. "I just want to (amase, amaze) your mom. She (loves, lovez) tomatoes."

Angela **giggled** as she started to (measure, meazure) the ground. "She sure (does, doez)," she said. "And she's going to love this (present, prezent). When it comes to gifts, you have great taste!"

★ **Spelling Bee Fun Fact** ★

In 1956, the winning word of the Scripps National Spelling Bee was *condominium*. A condominium is an apartment that is owned by the person who lives there. Most people shorten this word to *condo*. There are many words that are sometimes easier to use in a shorter form, like saying *mac* instead of *macaroni*. Can you think of a shorter way to say *vegetable*?

s versus z

In English, the letter *s* sometimes has a "z" sound when it follows a vowel. Good spellers know when to use each letter!

The following word search puzzle contains the correctly spelled *s* and *z* words from the story. Find all eleven words. Remember, if you can't find a word, you might be spelling it incorrectly.

Y	E	F	R	E	E	Z	E
J	N	T	N	S	Z	A	Z
D	C	R	M	I	I	R	A
I	N	E	E	R	S	L	M
C	S	A	A	P	U	O	A
L	E	S	S	R	P	V	S
F	Z	U	U	P	E	B
I	I	R	R	S	O	S	L
Y	R	E	E	D	S	H	V
C	P	R	E	S	E	N	T

Search for the correct spelling of each word:

1. treasure, treazure
2. suppose, suppoze
3. freese, freeze
4. surprise, surprize
5. measure, meazure
6. sise, size
7. thousand, thouzand
8. amase, amaze
9. loves, lovez
10. does, doez
11. present, prezent

Answers: 1. treasure, 2. suppose, 3. freeze, 4. surprise, 5. measure, 6. size, 7. thousand, 8. amaze, 9. loves, 10. does, 11. present

It's a Piece of Cake

Leah frowned at the cake sitting before her. She had tried her best, but it wasn't quite perfect. The frosting was all lumpy, especially on top of the cake.

"I'll **never** finish it in time for the party," she said with a sigh.

"Sure you will, Leah," said her mom, who had just come into the kitchen. "I know just how to fix it. We'll get that CAKE DONE!"

Leah's mom opened a drawer.

"It's a good thing I CAME in," she said, taking a utensil that looked like a rounded knife out of the drawer. "Frosting is tricky without the **necessary** tool. COME here, Leah, and let me show you."

Leah's mom held up the knife.

"This is a frosting spatula," she explained. "Watch what I do."

With a few careful swipes of the spatula, Leah's mom fixed the cake's lumpy frosting.

"See? This spatula made the cake's DOME nice and smooth," she said.

Leah clapped in **delight**. "It's DONE!" she cried.

"It sure is. I told you we'd get that CAKE DONE." Her mom grinned.

"You were right. It's absolutely perfect," Leah declared. "And the party will be perfect, too!"

Spelling Words

never	NEV-ur	*adverb*	not ever
necessary	NES-uh-sayr-ee	*adjective*	needed or required
delight	di-LAHYT	*noun*	joy

Word Ladders, #4

Leah's mom made a word ladder to change the word CAKE into DONE. Here is the word ladder:

CAKE – CAME – COME – DOME – DONE

Can you complete the following word ladders?

1. **MEAL** – _ _ _ _ – _ _ _ _ – **BELT**
2. **DESK** – _ _ _ _ – _ _ _ _ – **FISH**
3. **SOME** – _ _ _ _ – _ _ _ _ – **GOLD**

★ **Spelling Bee Fun Fact** ★

Baking is often described as a science, because you have to be extremely careful and precise to do it well. The 1950 Scripps National Spelling Bee winning word means that kind of attention to detail: *meticulosity* (muh-tik-yoo-LAH-si-tee). And it takes meticulosity to succeed at baking the 1970 winning word: *croissant*.

Answers:
1. MEAL – MEAT – MELT – BELT
2. DESK – DISK – DISH – FISH
3. SOME – SOLE – SOLD – GOLD

Fun-Sized

Imagine you were very small,
Smaller than a baby doll.
You'd see the world from way down **low**.
Your **shadow**, it would barely show.
You couldn't reach the pantry shelf.
At least, you couldn't by yourself!
You'd have to **borrow** something tall
To climb to anything at all.
Once you got there, don't you know,
The floor would be way down below.
The pantry would seem like a house
To you, as tiny as a mouse.
Scary? Maybe—but be glad!
'Cause being small is not all bad.
The food would all be giant size—
You'd never run out of supplies!

Spelling Words

low	loh	*adjective*	not far above the ground
shadow	SHA-doh	*noun*	a dark shape that appears on a surface when something blocks the light
borrow	BAHR-oh	*verb*	to use something that belongs to someone else

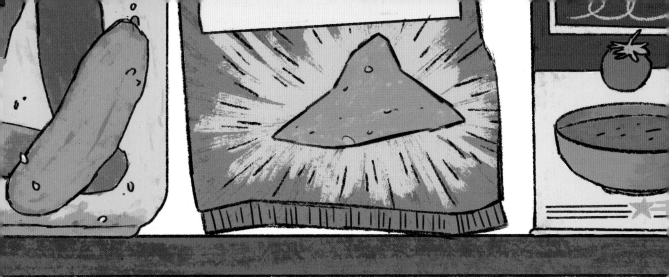

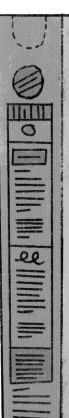

-ow Words

Many words in this poem end with the letter combination *ow*. The letter *w* is silent, so the combination makes an "oh" sound.

All of the words on this list end with an "oh" sound. Fill in the blanks with *o* or *ow* to complete the words.

1. tomat___
2. foll___
3. hipp___
4. sn___
5. mang___

6. gr___
7. avocad___
8. nach___
9. yell___
10. swall___

Dog Treats

Juan's family visited the farmers' market one Saturday afternoon. While his parents shopped, Juan munched on an apple and watched people walk by with their dogs. Juan wished he could have a pet, but his apartment building didn't allow them. Here, though, he could see big dogs, small dogs, happy dogs, and yappy dogs. They were all different. They were all great!

A beagle went past. The beagle had an enormous bow on her collar.

"That's **fancy**," Juan said.

Next came a greyhound wearing a sweater.

"Ooh! That's even fancier," Juan said.

Then Juan's eyes opened wide! He gazed in wonder at a poodle with a poofy haircut, a **dazzling** jeweled leash, and painted toenails.

"Wow! That's the fanciest dog for sure," Juan said.

"She *is* the fanciest," Juan's mom agreed. "She deserves a prize!"

"How about a treat?" Juan suggested. "Can we buy some? Please? For *all* the dogs?"

Juan's mom smiled. "Definitely! Just ask the owners first."

Juan grinned as he walked to a booth to buy dog biscuits. Fancy, fancier, or fanciest—it didn't matter. Today *all* the dogs were in for a treat!

★ **Spelling Bee Fun Fact** ★

The shortest winning word in the history of the Scripps National Spelling Bee was *luge* (loozh), in 1984. A luge is a sled that you ride lying on your back, feetfirst, down an icy track. In 2015, a record was broken for the longest championship word. Spelled with a whopping fifteen letters, *scherenschnitte* (SHAYR-un-shnit-uh) is the German art of cutting paper into beautiful, detailed designs.

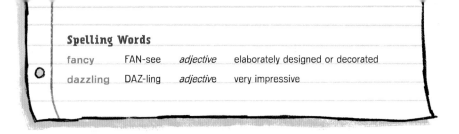

Spelling Words

| fancy | FAN-see | *adjective* | elaborately designed or decorated |
| dazzling | DAZ-ling | *adjective* | very impressive |

Comparatives and Superlatives

The word *fancier* is called a "comparative" because it compares things. (*This dog is fancier than that one.*) The word *fanciest* is called a "superlative" because it names the most extreme example of a thing. (*This dog is the fanciest.*) Change the *y* ending of an adjective to *-ier* and *-iest* to form comparatives and superlatives.

Can you spell the comparative and superlative of each of the following words?

1. **happy**   2. **funny**   3. **muddy**   4. **angry**

Answers: 1. happier, happiest; 2. funnier, funniest; 3. muddier, muddiest; 4. angrier, angriest

The Missing Ingredient

Lillian sighed. She had lots of homework tonight! She was writing a report about nutrition, and she had to do some online research. She wanted to read about balanced diets and healthy eating.

Lillian sat down at her dad's computer. The screen glowed as the computer turned on. A box appeared on the screen. *Password*, it requested.

"What's your password, Dad?" Lillian called to her father, who was working in another room.

"It's almost Halloween, so I just changed it to *pumpkin*," her father called back. He laughed. "I'm aware that it's silly, but I'm in a holiday mood!"

Lillian giggled as she typed the funny password into the box: P-U-M-K-I-N. She hit the enter key. Right away, a message popped up on the screen.

Incorrect password, it read. *Try again.*

"Dad?" Lillian called again. "It doesn't work."

"What? It should," her father replied. "Pumpkin. P-U-M-P-K-I-N."

"What? There's no middle *p* in *pumpkin*," said Lillian. She pronounced the word "pum-kin," just as her father had.

"There is a *p* in there, but a lot of people don't pronounce it," Lillian's father replied. "I guess I'm one of them. Apparently you are, too."

"Okay. Well, then, I made a spelling mistake," Lillian said. She typed again, just as her father had said: P-U-M-P-K-I-N. The computer hummed, and the main screen appeared.

"I'm in! Thanks, Dad," Lillian said. "Now I can do my homework. And since my homework is all about food, maybe I'll learn something about pumpkins. I know the correct spelling now, so that's a start!"

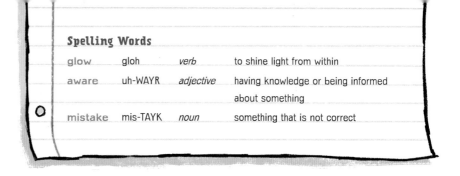

Spelling Words

glow	gloh	*verb*	to shine light from within
aware	uh-WAYR	*adjective*	having knowledge or being informed about something
mistake	mis-TAYK	*noun*	something that is not correct

Silent Letters

Some words, like *pumpkin*, contain letters that aren't always pronounced in speech. There's no good rule to help you understand these words. You just have to memorize them.

The following food words contain silent letters. The silent letters are missing! Choose the correct silent letters from the list to fill in each blank.

     b,   e,   g,   h,   h,   l,   p,   s

1. sa_mon
2. ras_berry
3. om_let
4. lam_
5. lasa_na
6. brussel_ sprout
7. r_ubarb
8. spag_etti

Answers: 1. l, 2. p, 3. e, 4. b, 5. g, 6. s, 7. h, 8. h

A Good Day for Ice Cream

Shanice and her friend Jonas were naming some of their favorite things.

"You know what I love? Sundaes," Shanice said. "They're the best!"

"How come?" Jonas replied.

"I guess it's sort of a family tradition," Shanice said. "We have sundaes together."

"Family time is the best," Jonas agreed. "What do you do?"

"Well," said Shanice, "we start with ice cream. Then we add chocolate syrup and whipped cream, piled **high**. We put cherries and nuts on top."

"Wow, you're so lucky!" said Jonas. "I hardly ever get ice cream. I can't believe you have it every week."

"What do you mean? We don't have it every week. My parents say it's a **privilege**. We earn it by getting good grades," said Shanice.

"But you said your family always has Sundays together, with ice cream," Jonas said.

"Aha! I understand now," Shanice said with a smile. "I was talking about S-U-N-D-A-E-S, not S-U-N-D-A-Y-S. Ice cream sundaes."

Jonas smiled, too.

"You know what would be REALLY great?" he said. "A sundae on a Sunday!"

"You're right!" Shanice replied. "It's nice to relax at the end of the week—and a sundae sure is a tasty way to celebrate!"

★ Spelling Bee Fun Fact ★

The Scripps National Spelling Bee's official dictionary lists more than 472,000 words. That's almost half a million! And English continues to add more words all the time, just like *sundae*. Have you ever had a *staycation* or watched a *webisode*? Those are both new words. A fancy word for "new words" is *neologisms* (nee-AH-luh-jiz-umz).

Deliberate Misspellings

People started using the word *sundae* after the sweet treat was invented in the 1800s. At this time, people began to enjoy ice cream treats on the last day of the week. They started calling them *Sundays*. Store owners changed the spelling, and the new spelling stuck.

Companies sometimes change the regular spelling of a product's name to make it stand out on the shelf. Even some foods have names that are deliberate misspellings. Here are a few examples. Can you spell each word correctly? Can you think of some other deliberate misspellings?

1. **Biskit**
2. **Froot**
3. **Krab**
4. **Kreme**
5. **Tastee**

Spelling Words			
high	hahy	*adjective*	far up off the ground
privilege	PRIV-lij	*noun*	a right or benefit that is an advantage for some people over others

Ari's Shopping List

It is Super Secret Letter Day again, and this time it is Ari's turn. Ari can only shop for things that contain a certain type of letter. Can you figure out what it is?

- ▶ He can buy an apple, but not a banana.
- ▶ He can buy sauce, but not gravy.
- ▶ He can buy lemonade, but not lemons.
- ▶ He can buy a sausage, but not a hot dog.
- ▶ He can buy a pickle, but not a cucumber.
- ▶ He can buy a vegetable, but not a fruit.
- ▶ He can buy **juice**, but not milk.
- ▶ He can buy a grape, but not a berry.
- ▶ He can buy a cantaloupe, but not a **watermelon**.
- ▶ He can buy an artichoke, but not a squash.

Ari just wants to know one thing: Is he allowed to buy a magazine to read while he eats? Why or why not? **Can you name the secret letter?**

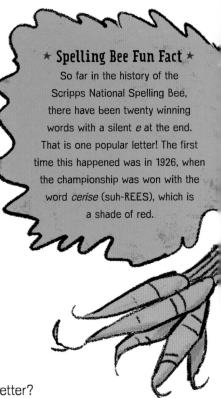

★ **Spelling Bee Fun Fact** ★
So far in the history of the Scripps National Spelling Bee, there have been twenty winning words with a silent *e* at the end. That is one popular letter! The first time this happened was in 1926, when the championship was won with the word *cerise* (suh-REES), which is a shade of red.

Spelling Words

juice	joos	*noun*	the liquid that comes from a plant, like a fruit or a vegetable
watermelon	WAH-tur-mel-un	*noun*	a sweet, juicy fruit with a green rind and usually pink or red pulp

Silent *e*

The silent *e* hangs around at the end of many English words. It doesn't have a sound of its own, but it has a few important jobs:

1. It can tell us to use a long vowel sound, as in *lime*.
2. It can tell us to use a soft consonant sound, as in *rice*.
3. It can just be there to add a vowel to the word's last syllable, as in *waffle*.

Look at the words from the story and then at the options above. Which job is the silent *e* doing in each word? Write 1, 2, or 3 in the blank.

1. **apple** _____
2. **sauce** _____
3. **lemonade** _____
4. **sausage** _____
5. **pickle** _____

6. **vegetable** _____
7. **juice** _____
8. **grape** _____
9. **cantaloupe** _____
10. **artichoke** _____

Answers: 1. apple 3; 2. sauce 2; 3. lemonade 1; 4. sausage 2; 5. pickle 3; 6. vegetable 3; 7. juice 2; 8. grape 1; 9. cantaloupe 1; 10. artichoke 1

Taste Test

Devin and Rafe were doing their homework one night when Rafe looked up from his science book. "It says here that it can be hard to identify flavors if you're blindfolded," he said.

"Let's try it!" Devin replied.

The boys trooped to the kitchen. Devin sat in a chair, and Rafe tied a bandanna across his eyes.

"Don't be afraid," Rafe said. "Here we go. Open up!"

Devin opened his mouth and Rafe popped something in. It was small, round, juicy, and sweet.

"Yum! It's a cherry," Devin said.

"Right!" said Rafe.

Next, Rafe gave Devin another food to try. This one was hard, crunchy, and salty.

"Easy! That's a peanut," Devin said.

"Right again!" said Rafe. "Let's try one more. Open wide."

This time, a liquid dripped onto Devin's tongue. The liquid was very sour.

"Ugh! That's lemon juice," Devin cried with a grimace.

Rafe laughed. "Right yet again. You're good at this, Devin!" he said.

"I guess anything is possible if you try hard enough." Devin laughed. "Although I have to say, it didn't seem all that hard to me. Maybe I'm a food genius. Now I've got to take this bandanna off and have a drink of water. I need to wash that sour taste out of my mouth!"

Spelling Words

| night | nahyt | *noun* | the time of darkness between one day and the next |
| enough | ee-NUF | *adverb* | in the amount needed |

Parts of Speech: Adjectives

Knowing a word's part of speech and definition can help you spell the word. An *adjective* is a word that describes a noun or a pronoun.

The story you just read contains five adjectives from the *Feed Me Words* Index of Spelling Words (pages 85–86). Match each adjective with its definition.

1. **sour**   a. able to happen or be done
2. **possible**   b. having an acidic taste like a lemon
3. **salty**   c. containing a lot of sugar
4. **sweet**   d. feeling fear
5. **afraid**   e. seasoned with salt

Answers: 1. b, 2. a, 3. e, 4. c, 5. d

Smells Like a Winner

One consonant or two? Choose the correctly spelled words as you read this story. The puzzle at the end will help you check your choices.

The (biter, bitter) smell hit Georgia the (moment, momment) she opened the **refrigerator**. "Ugh!" she cried. "Something in here is (roten, rotten)!"

Georgia started to move food around on the refrigerator shelves. There was a lot of food!

"There's so much (cluter, clutter)," Georgia grumbled. "I need to make some space."

Georgia started (puling, pulling) things out of the fridge. She emptied the whole top (level, levvel). She found some leftover (bacon, baccon) and a jar of (mayonaise, mayonnaise). But they smelled fine.

Next, Georgia moved down to the (second, seccond) shelf. She found a stray (lemon, lemmon) and half a (peper, pepper). But they smelled fine, too.

Georgia was about to start on the third shelf when her brother, Gary, entered the kitchen.

"Hey!" Gary cried. "Be careful! My entry for the **science** fair is in there!"

A science experiment? Hmm, could it be . . . ?

"What experiment did you choose for your entry, Gary?" Georgia asked (sweetly, sweetlly).

"I'm (roting, rotting) some eggs," Gary said proudly. "Can you tell?"

"I certainly can," Georgia answered, wrinkling her nose. "Well, at least now I know where that (awful, awfull) smell is coming from. I can stop looking . . . and you can take those eggs straight to the science fair. Your experiment smells like a winner to me!"

Spelling Words

refrigerator	ree-FRIJ-ur-ay-tur	*noun*	an appliance used to keep food and drinks cold
science	SAHY-en(t)s	*noun*	a branch of knowledge dealing with facts, truths, and natural laws

Double Consonants, #2

It can be really hard to remember when to use double or single consonants. This story gives you extra practice in this important skill.

The following word search puzzle contains the correctly spelled words from the story. Find all fourteen words. Remember, if you can't find a word, you might be spelling it incorrectly.

P	U	L	L	I	N	G	B	L	L
D	R	U	K	J	G	I	E	R	U
O	S	F	E	S	T	V	E	A	N
C	E	W	K	T	E	P	P	V	O
L	V	A	E	L	P	C	C	M	C
U	E	R	N	E	T	T	O	R	A
T	U	M	P	Y	T	M	R	N	B
T	Z	Z	O	U	E	L	X	H	D
E	S	I	A	N	N	O	Y	A	M
R	O	T	T	I	N	G	Q	V	K

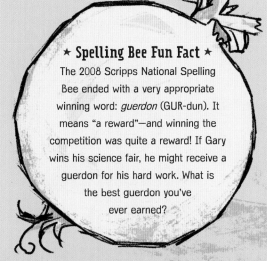

★ **Spelling Bee Fun Fact** ★

The 2008 Scripps National Spelling Bee ended with a very appropriate winning word: *guerdon* (GUR-dun). It means "a reward"—and winning the competition was quite a reward! If Gary wins his science fair, he might receive a guerdon for his hard work. What is the best guerdon you've ever earned?

Search for the correct spelling of each word:

1. biter, bitter
2. moment, momment
3. roten, rotten
4. cluter, clutter
5. puling, pulling
6. level, levvel
7. bacon, baccon
8. mayonaise, mayonnaise
9. second, seccond
10. lemon, lemmon
11. peper, pepper
12. sweetly, sweetlly
13. roting, rotting
14. awful, awfull

Answers: 1. bitter, 2. moment, 3. rotten, 4. clutter, 5. pulling, 6. level, 7. bacon, 8. mayonnaise, 9. second, 10. lemon, 11. pepper, 12. sweetly, 13. rotting, 14. awful

If Wishes Were Fishes

Will was shopping for groceries one day. He gazed hungrily at the display in the seafood department. The fresh fish looked delicious! Maybe he should buy some.

The clerk behind the counter saw Will looking at the fish. "Hello, **customer**! Would you like some FISH from the CASE?" he asked.

"Yes, please!" Will replied.

"Okay," said the clerk. "But we do things a little differently here. If you want FISH, first you have to WISH for it."

"Um, all right," Will said, puzzled. He closed his eyes. "I wish for some fish," he said out loud, pointing to a tasty fillet.

"Great. Now I WASH my hands," said the clerk. He rinsed his hands under a faucet, then held them out toward Will.

"CASH, please. That fillet costs five dollars," he said.

Will put the money into the clerk's clean hands. The clerk took the money and put it into the register. He slipped a pair of plastic gloves onto his hands.

"Now I open the CASE. I take the FISH from the CASE and put it into a bag . . . and then I give it to you!" he said, handing Will the bag of fish.

"Hooray! Fish for supper," said Will. "Thank you."

"It's my **pleasure**," replied the clerk. "I love to make people's wishes come true!"

Word Ladders, #5

The seafood clerk made a word ladder to change the word FISH into CASE. Here is the word ladder:

FISH – WISH – WASH – CASH – CASE

Can you complete the following tricky word ladders?

1. **MILK** – _ _ _ _ – _ _ _ _ – _ _ _ _ – **PINT**
2. **HATE** – _ _ _ _ – _ _ _ _ – _ _ _ _ – **LOVE**
3. **LAMB** – _ _ _ _ – _ _ _ _ – _ _ _ _ – **SOLE**

Good for You

Hunter read the next clue for the crossword puzzle he was working on: "13 Across, Broccoli is a common type," it said.

"That's easy! Broccoli is a vegetable," Hunter said.

Hunter found the correct space in the puzzle and started to enter the letters. V-E-G-T-A-B-L-E, he wrote. Then he frowned.

"Huh. There's still one empty space," he muttered. "But how can that be? I was positive I was right."

"Maybe you were," said Hunter's sister from across the room. "Why don't you look up the word in the dictionary?"

"Good idea," said Hunter. He got up, grabbed a dictionary from a shelf, and flipped to the V section.

"Here it is. V-E-G . . . Hey! There's a sneaky E after the G!" he cried.

Hunter erased the letters he had written on the puzzle and carefully reentered the word.

"V-E-G-E-T-A-B-L-E. That extra letter increased the word's length. Now it fits," he said happily. "I had the right idea, but the wrong spelling. I guess that's important for a puzzle, but not so much at the table. No matter how you spell them, vegetables are always delicious!"

Swallowed Syllables

A *syllable* is a word part with one vowel sound. It is sort of like a spoken "beat." Each word has a certain number of these beats. For instance, the word *number* has two beats: "num-ber." The word *syllable* has three: "syl-la-ble."

A swallowed syllable is one that looks like it should be pronounced when written, but often is not pronounced when spoken. The word *vegetable* is one example. It is usually pronounced "vej-table," not "vej-e-table."

When spoken, the words on the following list usually have swallowed syllables. Read each word out loud exactly as written. Then say the word like you would normally say it. Which syllables are swallowed?

1. **probably**
2. **every**
3. **different**
4. **temperature**
5. **Wednesday**
6. **family**

Spelling Words

common	KAH-mun	*adjective*	widespread or ordinary
empty	EMP-tee	*adjective*	not containing anything
increase	in-KREES	*verb*	to make larger in size or amount

Answer: The second syllable in each of these words is commonly swallowed.

Snack Attack

Little Joe awoke one night.
The house was dark; the moon was bright.
He heard a creak upon the stair.
What **creepy** thing might be out there?
Could it be a frightful beast
Hungry for a midnight feast?
Would it hear the slightest noise?
Would it **pounce** on sleepy boys?
Little Joe was full of fright
But ready to put up a fight!
Out of bed and to his door
Crept Little Joe across the floor.
With one yank, Joe's door
opened wide.
Joe's "monster" dad was right outside!
"Sorry, son. I had a snack."
He laughed, and Little Joe laughed back.
"These cookies that your mom just bought—
So good . . . so good! I guess I'm caught!"
"You scared me, Dad! I had a fright,
You were the monster in the night!!"
Dad quickly gave his son a hug,
While cookie crumbs fell to the rug.
"Come on, son, and help me out.
I'll give you one if you don't pout.
Let's get these cookies out of sight
And get you tucked in, nice and tight.
Since I'm the monster in your head,
It's time to get you back to bed."

-ght Words

Many words in this poem contain the *ght* combination. In this combination, the letters *gh* are silent. This means that the letters *ght* make a "t" sound.

All of the words on the following list end with a "t" sound. Fill in the blanks with *ght* or *t* to complete the words.

1. frui___
2. ei___
3. deli___
4. trea___
5. ki___
6. fou___
7. grea___
8. bai___
9. hei___
10. mea___
11. sou___
12. roo___

Spelling Words

| creepy | KREE-pee | *adjective* | disturbing or causing fear |
| pounce | pownts | *verb* | to jump suddenly |

About the
★ Scripps National Spelling Bee ★

Each year, millions of students across the country and around the globe come together to compete in classroom and school spelling bees. Of these millions, a fraction will move on to win regional bees and qualify for one of the approximately 280 coveted slots at the Scripps National Spelling Bee, held each May.

Most of the Scripps National Spelling Bee's annual participants are from the United States—but some have come from as far away as Japan, Ghana, and Guam. In order to be eligible to participate in the finals, students can be no more than fifteen years old and can not yet have graduated from the eighth grade. Additionally, previous winners are ineligible to compete again.

You may have seen the finals of the Scripps National Spelling Bee on television or online, but that's just one portion of an entire week of fun planned for the contestants in and around Washington, D.C. During Bee Week, the best spellers in the world come together to celebrate their achievements and make new friends, starting with a big family barbecue packed with great food, field games, dance-offs, and arts and crafts. Every speller is treated like a celebrity—or, as we like to say, a "spellebrity"—and is given an autograph book called the *Bee Keeper* for collecting as many signatures as possible from fellow contestants.

The spellers also have the opportunity to explore Washington, D.C., together and see some of our nation's most significant historic sites and spectacles. And at the end of the week, there's a formal awards banquet followed by a dance party to give spellers the chance to bid farewell to their 280 new friends.

During the week, contestants regularly have the opportunity to give candid on-camera interviews with local and national reporters, showing off their love for and mastery of words. This gets them used to the limelight for the competition itself! However, there are multiple rounds of the competition that spellers must tackle before the big nationally televised semifinals and finals.

The competition kicks off with the Preliminaries Test, which consists of both spelling and vocabulary components. Points are awarded for correct answers, and a contestant can earn up to thirty points during this phase of the competition.

Rounds Two and Three follow the Preliminaries Test and consist of oral spelling on stage. Each correct spelling in these rounds is worth three points, and contestants who misspell their words are eliminated from the competition. At the end of Round Three, points are tallied, and up to fifty of the top-scoring spellers move on to the finals.

During the finals, contestants spell words orally on stage, just like in Rounds Two and Three. Any one of the more than 470,000 words in the dictionary is fair game for the competition.

As these finalists go head-to-head on stage for the national title, there are two rules they must keep in mind: they must spell their word within two minutes from when it is first pronounced, and they may not change their spelling at any point. They may, however, ask the official pronouncer for the word's definition, part of speech, language(s) of origin, and alternate pronunciation(s). They can also ask to hear the word in a sentence and whether they've correctly identified the word's root(s). All of these factors may help a speller determine how to spell a word—and many contestants study other languages in order to make educated guesses about the spelling of unfamiliar words.

Throughout all of this, the stage is surrounded by television cameras for the national broadcast, as well as hundreds of reporters eager to tell the stories of the champions. Everyone is there to cheer the contestants on.

Want to Spell at This Mic Someday?

With some persistence and resourcefulness, it just might happen! All you need to do is become a word collector, just like some kids become toy or rock or coin collectors.

Great additions to your collection are everywhere. For example, if you want to collect food words, flip through your family's cookbooks. Or write down all the new words you see at the grocery store. The produce section and the spice aisle are especially interesting. And restaurant menus are great resources, too—just be sure to check the spelling in the dictionary when you get home.

Read, read, and then read some more. Add to your word collection by looking up and writing down the definitions of words that are new to you.

You can also practice with mini spelling bees at home. Try this: have a friend, family member, or teacher choose a book, magazine, newspaper, or website that you haven't seen, and quiz you on words selected from it randomly. The more you practice spelling, the more confident a speller you will be.

The journey to the Scripps National Spelling Bee starts right where you are: at home or in the classroom, with a list of words and a dream. To learn how to get started in spelling competitions, visit spellingbee.com today!

Index of Sidebars

Index of Spelling Words

Index of Spelling Words *(cont'd.)*